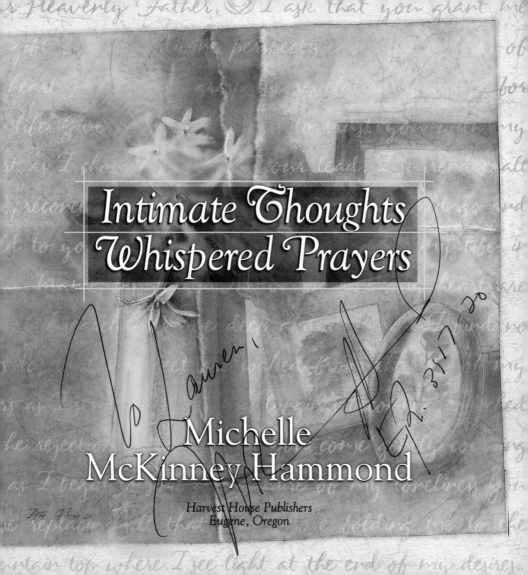

Intimate Thoughts Whispered Prayers

Michelle McKinney Hammond

Harvest House Publishers
Eugene, Oregon

Intimate Thoughts, Whispered Prayers
Text Copyright © 2001 Michelle McKinney Hammond
Artwork Copyright © 2001 Katia Andreeva
Published by Harvest House Publishers
Eugene, OR 97402

Published in association with the literary agency of Alive Communications, Inc.,
7680 Goddard Street, Suite 200, Colorado Springs, CO 80920

McKinney Hammond, Michelle, 1957-
    Intimate thoughts, whispered prayers / Michelle McKinney Hammond.
        p. cm.
    ISBN 0-7369-0528-6
    1. Single women—Prayer books and devotions—English. I. Title.

    BV4596.S5 M346 2001
    242'.6432—dc21   2001016948

Other Books by Michelle McKinney Hammond

What to Do Until Love Finds You
Secrets of an Irresistible Woman
His Love Always Finds Me
The Power of Femininity
Get a Love Life
If Men Are Like Buses Then How Do I Catch One?
Prayer Guide for the Brokenhearted
What Becomes of the Brokenhearted
How to Be Blessed and Highly Favored

To correspond with Ms. McKinney Hammond, write to: HeartWing Ministries, P.O. Box 11052,
Chicago, IL 60611; or email her at heartwingmin@yahoo.com. For speaking engagement inquiries
contact: Speak Up Speaker Services, 1-888-870-7719.

Design and production by Koechel Peterson and Associates, Minneapolis, Minnesota

Verses are from the Holy Bible, New International Version®. Copyright © 1973, 1978, 1984 by the
International Bible Society. Used by permission of Zondervan Publishing House.

Verses marked ASV are from the American Standard Version of the Bible.

Printed in Hong Kong.

01 02 03 04 05 06 07 08 09 10 / NG / 10 9 8 7 6 5 4 3 2 1

This one is dedicated to my One True Love—
The One who has never failed or forsaken me,
The One who gives me the desires of
my heart and every perfect gift,
The Ultimate Bridegroom and standard for every man—
Jesus Christ, the perfect picture of love Himself.

To my Harvest House family
(and believe me, you are family to me)—
Your prayers, support, and encouragement
cause me to fly ever higher.
I love and appreciate you all
more than you will ever know.
Thanks to Katia, for bringing my thoughts
to such beautiful life.

Forgive me

for overhearing your longings
and daydreams and making them public.
But perhaps my desire to let you know that you are not alone
in your inner quest overrode my usual sense of convention.
I have whispered the same words in the night,
had the identical conversations with friends,
and arrived at one thunderous conclusion:
The hole in our heart is not a person-sized hole.
It is a purpose-sized hole. Small wonder
we've had trouble filling the void—
it is far too large for one man to fill!

So if our purpose is not embracing a physical man, what is it?
Our purpose is to love and serve Him who created our hearts
in a shape to accommodate Himself. But what does that
have to do with having a physical lover? Ah, my sister, don't fret,
for when we do this one marvelous thing, the love will come.

Michelle McKinney Hammond

Take Me...

Sometimes I feel...

Sometimes I feel...
Sometimes I wonder
aloud and within

trying to find the certainty

of my tomorrows

and as I grope in the dark for a string

to turn the light on

my hands find nothing to grasp

yet I know it's there
eluding my heart

challenging me simply to trust

and keep coming

keep coming to you...

challenging me

Dear Heavenly Father,

I ask that You grant me the gift of Your divine perspective on the affairs of the heart. Help me to grasp the revelation of Your design for my life. Give me a willingness to trust You with my heart as I choose to follow Your lead. I surrender all of my preconceived notions of how my life should unfold and yield to Your perfect way and timing for my life, in Jesus' Name. *Amen.*

You come

The valley and my heart are one
as I search for love
deep and unending
I find no stair to climb
my feet are soaked
from the rain of my tears
as I stroll through my longings
becoming drenched
in the rejection of others
and You come
gently covering me as I begin
to sink in the mire of my loneliness
You come
replacing all that was before
folding me inside your heart
carrying me to the mountaintop
where I see light
at the end of my
desires...

Dear Heavenly Father,

Far too many times I have been tempted to take matters into my own hands when I don't see You coming through according to my schedule. Forgive me. Silence my fears and my doubt with Your Word. Holy Spirit, speak peace to my soul. Lord, help my unbelief and carry me toward Your promise as I learn to rest in You, in Jesus' Name. Amen.

from Your heart

You will never leave me or forsake me

these words sound strangely familiar

said by far too many

who didn't keep their promise

yet for every time I think You gone

I find You nearer than I thought

firmly rooted in the center of Your promise

"I will never leave you or forsake you..."

from Your heart

to my understanding...

never leave

Dear Heavenly Father,

Forgive me for ignoring You and seeking my comfort from others. Help me to find my fulfillment in You rather than in seeking it from those who can never deliver. Silence the lie of the enemy in my ears that tells me I am not desirable, not wanted, not loved. Send me Your comfort and teach me to bask in Your love. Fill every space of my soul with more of Yourself. Let me find in Your promises the refuge I mistakenly seek in the arms of others, in Jesus' Name. *Amen.*

What He does best

It is in the valley,

in the alone

that we find ourselves

in the best of company...

this is the place where

God fills all the empty spaces

for He has finally been

given the room

to do

what He does best...

in the valley

Dear Heavenly Father,

I know that you have promised that You are with me always, but yet I must confess that there are times when loneliness overwhelms me and I question Your nearness. I wonder how long this season of my life will last. I yearn to find a resting place for my longings. Please reveal Yourself and take me to a place that is higher than my desires. Teach me to finally release my heart into Your hands, in Jesus' Name. *Amen.*

This place
called alone

This place called alone

is not kind to my spirit's expectations

and I am lost in the prison of myself

while You patiently hold the key and

wait

wait for me

to invite You into this alone

place...

wait for me

Dear Heavenly Father,

Come in and be my heart's guest.
Fill it with Your overwhelming presence. Help me
to lay my expectations upon the altar of Your tender
hands. Draw me to You and hold me there. Free me
from the tangled web of my fears and dissatisfaction.
Be my fulfillment. Be the lover of my soul, but most
of all be my contentment, in Jesus' Name. *Amen.*

My flesh and my spirit

My flesh and my spirit war
  playing dangerous games with my heart
and I strain to hear Your voice above its demands
 I press
  I strain
I strive with myself
  until my weariness
    forces me to discover
      the only place
    of sweet and silent refuge
      is on my knees...

Oh, Lord,

Why is it that You are the last one I seek when I am in this place? Why do I struggle with what I can't fix? Perhaps I avoid Your presence because of my fear of what You will reveal to me. Yet when I finally drop my guard and listen to Your sweet and gentle whisper I am consumed by Your grace and Your peace. In spite of my childish ramblings, don't stop wooing me. Overtake me with Your Spirit and cover me with Your banner of love, in Jesus' Name. *Amen.*

I stand in the cold

I stand in the cold

shivering beneath the cloak of my doubt

and desperation

torn by the reality

of how little I trust You

as my stomach knots in hunger

for one word of reassurance

from You who holds the key

to my wholeness

that I'm really not alone...

reassurance

Dear Heavenly Father,

Why is it so difficult to trust You?

Your Word says that the just shall live by faith, but still I continually walk by what I see and stumble over its temporal evidence. Help me to see things from Your point of view—to know and understand that my future is hidden inside of Your love for me. Grant me the eyes of Your Spirit to see the pleasures at Your right hand that You have ordained for me, in Jesus' Name. *Amen.*

Sometimes I trip over hope

and in the midst of trying to regain my balance

I am propelled forward

into the arms of promise

where joy takes me by surprise

But sometimes hope

becomes a long winding road

that disappears over the horizon line

of my dreams and desires

and I am left wandering aimlessly

past my finite understanding

holding my trembling heart in my hands

daring to defy my rationalizations

and simply trust

hoping against hope

based on that one promise

that where there is God

there is hope...

Dear God,

Help me to rehearse Your Word more than my questions. Grant me the eyes of Your Spirit to see past that which my flesh points to. Open my ears to hear your whisper above the din of my vocal expectations. Open my hands to release all that keeps me from receiving Your joy. Your peace. My understanding of Your plan for me and the rest that brings as once again You become my hope, in Jesus' Name. *Amen.*

For I know the plans

For I know the plans
I have for you, saith the Lord
promises, promises
surely goodness and mercy shall follow you
all the days of your life...
promises, promises
He satisfies your desires with good things
promises, promises
He is able to do exceedingly, abundantly, above
all that you could ask or think
promises, promises
from God's lips
to my ears
to my heart...

May our Lord Jesus Christ himself and God our Father, who loved us and by his grace gave us eternal encouragement and good hope, encourage your hearts and strengthen you in every good deed and word.

—2 THESSALONIANS 2:16,17

my life. Give me a willingness to trust you wi
heart as I choose to follow your lead. I
my preconceived notion of
ield to your perfect way and timing
Jesus name. Amen. ♡ The valley
e as I search for love deep and
enter my heart
tain to climb my feet are soaked
ears as I stroll through my longings
the rejection of others and you
me as I begin to sink in the mire of
me replacing all that was before
ountain top where I see light at the end of my

Make Me...

I stand poised

I stand poised in expectation

awaiting that which my eyes haven't

seen

my ears haven't heard

that which has yet to enter my heart

and surpasses my imaginations

promises from God Himself

in exchange for my love

I stand

I wait

I expectantly watch

refusing to be moved by what I see

I stand

with my hands open

silently rehearsing His promises

for when I know nothing else

I know that God cannot lie...

Dear Father,

As I cling to Your promises, make them real to me. Let them be more than words that I rehearse. Make them the foundation of my trust. Increase my love for You that my faith might be unshakeable. Help me to keep my eyes on You. Still my heart and reassure my impatience that Your promises are never late, in Jesus' Name. *Amen.*

I hold my breath

I realize I have no choice but to wait

wait for the fulfillment of my expectations

and so with one eye on my desires

and the other eye on God

I hold my breath

and struggle to keep my feelings at bay

straining against the temptation

to race ahead of Him who holds my future

I peek around the folds of His robe

straining to capture a glimpse of what lies ahead

and I feel what I feel

whether imagined or real

the questions and answers remain the same

with a consistent bottom line

God is still on the throne

race ahead

Dear Heavenly Father,

As I yield to Your Lordship,

teach me Your ways. Grant me the understanding of Your purposes and the will to allow You to have Your way. Help me to pursue the desires of Your heart rather than my own personal longings. Turn my eyes and my heart toward the fulfillment of my destiny and fill me with the joy of being in the center of Your plan, in Jesus' Name. *Amen.*

Perhaps I have reached

Perhaps I have reached

and grasped for something I

was not prepared to hold

in my pursuit of a good thing

I forsook seeking the good in me

and created a void too cavernous
for a man to fill

and I am finally forced to carry my empty hands

and leaking heart

back to God...

in my pursuit

Dear Lord,

Prepare me to be a good thing

for the man that You have chosen for my life. But
more importantly still, cause me to walk in fulfillment where I am right now. Fill me with a sense of
purpose that causes me to celebrate each day. Let my
strength come from the joy that You alone can give,
in Jesus' Name. *Amen.*

I stand ashamed

I stand ashamed
of all that I still withhold from Him
and I am challenged
to forsake
everything that I consider safe…
my yearnings
race ahead of my suspicious will
throwing caution to the wind
provoking me to release all that I am
and surprisingly I find I've lost nothing
and found everything in the discovery
that the real comfort zone
is in the center of God's will…

provoking me

Dear Heavenly Father,

So many times in the past
I have superimposed my own desire over Yours.
And when I lose You in the midst of all my heart's
demands, I return to this place of realizing that it is
You who is truly in the center of my joy, in spite of
all I gain. Forgive me for assuming that You are here
to serve my purposes versus me serving Yours.
Thank You for waiting until I unfold my hands in
complete surrender to You. I now release all that I
hold dear and choose to grasp only what You offer,
in Jesus' Name. *Amen.*

Like a butterfly

Like a butterfly

fighting for a new tomorrow

I stretch within myself

struggling to unfold wings

that have been folded inward for far too long

and strength comes in the reaching

past where my heart has been

I fly

I soar

as I discover the joy of giving

on the other side of me...

joy of giving

Dear Lord,

Please pull me out of self

and into Your service. Help me to love those who are available to be loved and blessed by me. Show me those who have needs around me that I can fill. Help me as I give my life away to find a new dimension of fulfillment as I honor You through reaching out to others. Fill every empty place in my life with Your purposes and Your desires for me, in Jesus' Name. *Amen.*

"I love you..."

"I love you..."
"I want to share my forever with you..."
"Will you be mine?"
words I long to hear
said by the right one
in the right place
at the right time
yet for now my dreams elude me
leaving space for God to replace them
with visions of His own
and so my heart closes its eyes
and embraces new hopes
that live beyond the realm of my flesh...

Dear Lord,

Give me a heart that wants what You want, and give me the discernment to know the difference. Help me to quiet the insistence of my flesh that I might hear Your direction and not fall prey to neediness. Show me my weaknesses and be strong on my behalf. Grant me knowledge and understanding. Help me to walk in wisdom, leaving behind the mistakes of my past. Make my heart sound and establish me in Your love, in Jesus' Name. *Amen.*

warm and sweet

Tucked beneath the arm of God

warm and sweet

my heart finds a place where I can lay my weariness

and unanswerable questions

finding revelation in the rest

that His heartbeat gives

as I burrow deeper into the folds of His breast

lost in the depths of His mysteries

and riches untold

found in His love that

always fills me with more than I hoped for...

Dear Lord,

Help me to remain in Your lap, wrapped in Your arms, as I wait for the appointed day of my mate's arrival. Grant me the insight to consider through Your eyes the men I encounter. Keep me ever aware of Your presence and plan for my life. Help me not to settle for anything less than Your perfect design of love for me. Keep me in all my ways that I might be a woman who is a credit to Your kingdom. And prepare me for the one whom You will send, in Jesus' Name. *Amen.*

I rise

I rise

leaving all that is not like Him behind

washing myself in His Word

**anointing myself
with the balm of His Spirit**

until its aroma fills the air

intoxicating my senses with His goodness

filling me to overflowing
with the joy of living

and loving

and leaving tears behind...

Dear Lord,

Dress me in the beauty of Your holiness.

Let me never rely on the temporary outer adorning that the world sees as attractiveness, but instead on the quiet beauty of a yielded life to You. Let Your glory rest on me as I walk obediently before You. As I walk before You, help me to be blessed by being a blessing to others, and let my beauty be a reflection of You in all that I do, in Jesus' Name. *Amen.*

a season of the soul

I have found that the alone place

is no more than my personal winter

where all that is me dies

a season of the soul

pressed between the tendency

of my flesh and my heart to measure time

and so I wait for spring

and the warmth of the Son to release me

I turn my face to Him

and throw my arms open, surrendering to the light

until I find myself basking in His love

reveling in the alone times...

And ye shall be holy unto me: for I, Jehovah,
am holy, and have set you apart from
the peoples, that ye should be mine.

—LEVITICUS 20:26 ASV

...y life. Give me a willingness to trust you wit

...eart as I choose to follow your lead. I surre

...y preconceived notions of how my life should

...ield to your perfect way and timing for

...Jesus Name. Amen. ♡ The valley and my

...e as I search for love deep and

...air to climb my feet are soaked from the

...ears as I stroll through my longing for

...the rejection of others and you

...e a I begin to sink in the

...me replacing all that was before folding

...ountain top where I see light at the end of my

work in progress

love again

my heart

work of art

the Saviors hands

Whole...

I look in the mirror

I look in the mirror

and see a work in progress

a woman who has loved and lost

yet is willing to love again

I gaze at my heart

taking in its remains

and view an intricate reconstruction

wrought by the Savior's hands

and so I smile at the woman

who I will become

whole, free, and triumphant

I await the unveiling

of a finished work of art...

willing to love

Dear Heavenly Father,

This day I resubmit my life to you.

I ask that You dismantle every previous dream and goal that I have clung to that is not of You and replace it with Your vision for my life. I ask that You reveal Your ordained purpose for my life and give me the courage to follow it through. Fill my life with Yourself; fill every empty space in me with a sense of divine purpose and love for You. Let Your joy overflow in my heart and emanate from my soul as I bask in the knowledge that I am in the center of Your will, in Jesus' Name. *Amen.*

into Your love

I want to slide into Your love

   like a familiar foot

      slides into a pair of broken-in shoes

   and revel in the comfort of You...

      Your warmth

         Your softness

   Your quiet strength

      Your realness

I want to wrap myself tight in Your arms

   and dream a million dreams of You and me

   finally united for eternity

      in the light of Your glorious presence

      where all wrongs

         will be righted once and for all...

where all tears will turn to diamonds

and all trials will be fashioned into gold

where tribulations will emerge as jewels

to cast at Your feet...

I want to sink into You like a good down bed

and lose myself in the folds
of Your infinite care for me

never coming up for air...

safe

complete

ignoring the cold outside

I'm finally home...

lose myself

Drawing closer

I am drawing closer
　　to a place called love
　　　　　and it warms my heart
　　　even from here
I can see its flames rising in the distance
　　　not so far
　　drawing closer
I see no face to attach to my longing
　　and yet I know
　　that when I'm close enough
　　　I will see Him...

my heart

Dear Lord,

As I commit my heart into Your care, keep it safe within Your hands in accordance with Your Word. Teach me how to draw near to You. As I give my hopes and expectations to You, heal me and grant me the desires of my heart as You have promised. Be my comfort, my confidant, and my guide. Lead me to the place that is higher than my eyes can see. Show me the beauty of drawing near to You and the peace and fulfillment that can be found in making You the center of my joy, in Jesus' Name. *Amen.*

When I rise

When I rise full of love

for life and laughter

and the me that I am

love will meet me...

When I rise above my own neediness

fears and frustrated tears

and allow myself

to be warmed by the Son

love will shine on me

Yes, I will rise

and embrace love

consuming all that it contains

delighting myself in the fatness of my soul...

delighting me

Dear Heavenly Father,

Thank You for the precious gift of Your love.
Thank You for showing me what love looks like through the gift of Your Son. Grant me the gift of discernment to see the hidden motives of the hearts of men who enter my life so that I may not be deceived by the crumbs the enemy offers. Help me to wait on You to bring the one who will manifest Your love to me in human form. Until then, keep my heart in the palm of Your hand for safekeeping, in Jesus' Name. *Amen.*

I move

  even paced

head high

shoulders back

  feet firmly in place

    making choices from my head not my heart

ignoring the demands of the flesh

    I stretch my spirit and respond to God's voice

  running eagerly toward His instruction

caught up in His potent promises

I am bound to Him

a willing love slave

  yet freer than I've ever been...

Lord,

I come before you now,

laying all my insistences to rest. Here, take my heart and keep it. Guard it with the diligence I should have. Take my love and make it Yours. Take my arms and hold them. I choose to bind myself to the horns of Your altar and refuse to let go until You bless me with the fulfillment of wholeness in You. Wash me and dress me in the beauty of Your holiness and make me a worthy bride in Your eyes, in Jesus' Name. *Amen.*

I rest in the knowledge that Your wings

will carry me to a place called faith

and deliverance

a place where lies whispered in the dark

must flee in the face of such intense light

for this is a place where God is

and love dwells

for God and love are one...

drawing me ever higher

chains snapping from my heart

my mind

my soul

I soar ever higher

carried on the wings of love itself

until I reach a place where joy welcomes me

and whispers I am safe...

Dear Heavenly Father,

I now submit my spirit, my will, and my mind to You. Take them and transform them into the original image of the woman You created me to be. Renew me by the transforming power of Your Word. Grant me insight into Your design for love and free me from self-defeating habits. Expose every blind spot and area of denial in my heart. Free me to give and receive love as never before, in Jesus' Name. *Amen.*

I lie content in the arms of my Savior
letting Him rock me
and love me
like no lover can…

and I learn of love
of life and giving…

and I wait…
clear-eyed
with no misguided expectations
no desperate desires
no distorted views
binding me and marring my judgment

I sigh
and sink ever deeper into His lap
knowing He is able to keep
what I've placed in His care
and that all of my tomorrows
will be only what He has planned…

Dear Heavenly Father,

I submit my body to You.

I ask Your Holy Spirit to rise up in me and equip
me to keep myself holy and set apart unto You.
Help me to value my body as You value it. Help
me to please Your heart more than the flesh of man.
Keep me unto the day when You will smile upon
my union with the one whom You have chosen for
me. Let the vision of what You have in store for me
establish my resolve to wait until it is permissible
to share my love in intimacy with another, in
Jesus' Name. *Amen.*

As I press past

As I press past selfish dreams and ambitions
retrieving the pearls
I foolishly cast before swine
no longer weeping over
the trampled pieces of my heart
now restored to give again
to one more deserving
I discover that I am
lost in Him
only to be found in the truth
stronger than ever
ready to love better
because I now have more to give
and I will give it carefully
abundantly
only at His leading
understanding so much more
now that I have embraced this feeling
called wholeness...

Dear Heavenly Father,

I come to you seeking total restoration with You.
Today I would like to reestablish a love covenant
between us. I want to stand before You completely
whole and unashamed, free to share all that I am
with You. Thank You for first loving me. Thank You
for giving Your Son just for me. As I seek to draw
closer to You, meet me and unfold Your nature and
Your ways to me, that I might grow ever more intimate with You as I increase in the knowledge of who
You are, in Jesus' Name. *Amen.*

Here I stand

Here I stand radiating love
free at last

whole enough to hold that which is given
from the Master's hand

secure enough to let go of it all
He asks me to release
and yet my hands are full
as is my heart and my soul
a vessel no longer broken
containing all that is good
rich provisions of peace
and joy unspeakable
that I am free
to bid others to come
and drink from my brimming cup
to partake of my love offerings
for I have plenty to spare...

This much I've learned is true
timing is everything
purpose is supreme
and surrender
is only the beginning...

I am free

Dear Father,

I finally trust You.

You have proven Yourself faithful, and so I will wait.
I will wait for You. I will look for You as You come
bearing promises of to have and to hold forever and
ever, amen. For You are my knight, my prince, my
king. As I become one with You, I find I lack no
good thing. I accept Your good and perfect gifts and
choose to walk in the purpose for which I was
created. I will celebrate Your love for me, for none is
truer. And so I give You all of me in exchange for all
of You, and I rest in the completion that Your love
brings, in Jesus' Name. *Amen.*

Our Love Covenant

On this very day, <u>July 5, 2002</u>,

I pledge my covenant of renewed love to You,

O Lord—from this day forward to love, to trust, to

obey, even as I wait, forevermore.

Lauren Jo Singleton
(your signature here)

As a bridegroom rejoices over his bride,
so will your God rejoice over you.

ISAIAH 62:5

Forevermore